Look around you
Farm

Ruth Thomson

Photography by Chris Fairclough

WAYLAND

First published in 2007 by Wayland

Copyright © Wayland 2007

Wayland
338 Euston Road
London NW1 3BH

Wayland Australia
Level 17/207 Kent Street
Sydney, NSW 2000

Editor: Victoria Brooker
Designer: Elaine Wilkinson
Concept design: Paul Cherrill
Consultant: George Harcourt, Hard Farm, Field Dalling, Norfolk

British Library Cataloguing in Publicaton Data

Thomson, Ruth
On a farm. – (Look around you)
        1. Farms – Juvenile literature 2. Farm life –
        Juvenile literature 3. Human ecology – Juvenile literature
        I. Title
        910.9'1734

ISBN 978 0 7502 5146 4

For use of additional photographs, the author and publisher would like to thank:
©A ROOM WITH VIEWS/Alamy for the picture page 16 (bottom) and
© Rob Cousins/ Alamy for the picture page 17 (middle).

Printed in China

Wayland is a division of Hachette Children's Books.

# Contents

Words in **bold** can be found in the glossary.

Farms everywhere

Farmers use land to grow crops and keep animals. Cereal farms grow grains, such as wheat. Some farms grow vegetables and fruit.

Dairy farms keep cows for milk. Beef and pig farms raise animals for their meat. Sheep are kept for their meat and their wool. Poultry farms rear chickens for eggs and meat. Mixed farms grow crops and raise animals.

▲ Beef farms are the most common type of farm in Britain.

▼ This dairy farm is surrounded by grassy fields, divided by hedges and trees.

▲ Sheep graze on moorlands in the north of England.

LOOK CLOSER!

Find out what farmers produce in the area where you live.

Tomatoes

Sprouts

Plums

◀ Apples, plums and pears are grown in **orchards**. The trees are planted in rows to make picking easier.

▶ This farmer grows vegetables on flat and **fertile** land.

▲ Salad crops are often grown inside large, warm glasshouses.

Cereal farms

Wheat

In the autumn, cereal farmers plough the soil. They use a cultivator to break up the soil even more and a drill to plant wheat or oat seeds. As crops grow, they are sprayed to kill weeds and **pests,** and fed with **fertiliser**. In late summer, the grains are ripe. A combine harvester cuts them.

Grains are used for breakfast cereals or to make flour for bread and pasta. Some are used as animal feed.

The plough turns over the soil into long **furrows**.

Seeds are blown down the thin tubes of this drill into the ground. The drill rakes soil over the seeds, so birds do not eat them.

A combine harvester separates the grain from the straw. The grain is poured into a trailer. The straw is collected and made into **bales** for animal bedding.

Wheat grows in enormous flat fields where it is easy for machines to work.

LOOK CLOSER!

Look in a shop to see how many products you can find made from wheat, oats and rye.

Vegetable crops

Some farmers grow vegetables, such as potatoes, carrots, leeks and cauliflowers. The seeds are planted in rows so that the crops grow to an even size and shape, and are easy to harvest.

Animal farmers grow fields of grass and turnips, swedes and beet to feed their animals in winter.

▲ Cauliflowers are cut by hand. They are put onto a moving belt and packed in a trailer.

LOOK CLOSER!

Find out what vegetables are grown near where you live.

Broccoli

Leeks

Potatoes

Cauliflower

Carrots

Onions

▲ Fields of grass are cut on hot days in June and turned to help it dry. The dried grass, known as hay, is made into **bales**.

▶ Sheep are given hay in winter when there is not enough grass for them to eat.

Turnips

Swede

◀ Swedes and turnips are some of the crops that farmers grow. These are often fed to animals, but they are also good for people to eat.

9

Dairy farms

Dairy farmers keep cows for milk. The milk can be made into butter, cheese, cream, ice cream and yogurt.

The cows live outdoors from late spring until early autumn. They graze on grass, so most dairy farms are in wet areas where grass grows quickly.

▼ Cows **produce** milk once they have had a calf. Calves are taken away from their mothers after a few days so the cows can be milked.

▲ Friesian cows produce the most milk.

▲ Jersey cows produce very creamy milk.

▶ Cows are milked twice a day – once early in the morning and again in the late afternoon.

◀ To help cows make more milk, they are fed special food in a feeding station, like this.

LOOK CLOSER!

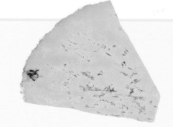

How many different milk products do you eat?

How many can you find in a shop?

Beef farms

Cattle such as Hereford and Charolais are kept for their meat, known as beef. In spring, the cattle graze on grass.

Over winter, they live in sheltered yards. They are fed on turnips, beet, **cattle cake**, hay and **silage** that the farmer has grown.

Prize-winning Hereford bulls are used for breeding better cattle.

A beef calf stays with its mother for eight months, before it is **weaned**.

Some beef cattle live on low hills in Wales, Scotland and Northern Ireland. Others live on rich **pastures** in Devon and the Midlands.

At around two years, the cattle are taken to market to be sold.

LOOK CLOSER!

Cattle live on low hills and rich pastures all over the country. Find out what kind of cattle live on a farm near you.

Sheep farming

There are many different **breeds** of sheep that farmers can keep. Each has been bred to survive in a particular area.

Hill sheep roam the rocky hills in the north and west of Britain. They have long, rough hair to protect them from the cold winters and wet weather. Lowland sheep are larger and have shorter, thicker wool.

▲ Hill sheep

▼ Lambs are born in winter and early spring. The lambs stay with their mother until they are sold in the summer.

▲ Lowland sheep

Farmers round up hill sheep on quad bikes for **dipping**, **shearing** or to move them to new **pastures**.

▲ Sheep are dipped like this, to kill the **parasites** that live on them.

▲ Once a year, sheep are sheared so that the wool can be used.

LOOK CLOSER!

Wool is washed, spun and knitted or woven into clothes. Find out what else wool is used for.

Chickens and pigs

Hens that lay eggs are sometimes kept indoors. Farmers check light, temperature and food to help the hens lay more eggs. Free range hens are allowed to wander outdoors.

Pigs are raised both indoors and outdoors. Indoor pigs are kept warm and fed on grain.

▲ Free range chickens are also fed grain, but scratch for worms and seeds too.

▼ Hundreds of chickens are kept together in big sheds and are fed grain every day.

LOOK CLOSER!

Look on egg boxes to see if the eggs inside are free range.

HAPPY HENS
LAYMORE EGGS
FREE
RANGE
EGGS
SOLD
HERE

▶ Mother pigs give birth to as many as ten piglets at a time. The piglets suck their mother's milk.

◀ Some pigs live outdoors with a hut to sleep in. They search for food themselves, as well as being fed.

Visiting a farm

Many farmers earn extra money from running a farm shop selling their own **produce**. They may offer bed and breakfast in their farmhouse or turn empty barns into places where holidaymakers can stay.

Some farms are open to visitors, so people can see how a farm is run. These often have special attractions, such as rides, tearooms or a pet corner.

▲ Some farmers plant fruit and vegetables for visitors to pick themselves.

▼ Visitors can watch these Gloucester Old Spot piglets at a farm that keeps rare breeds of animals.

This barn has been turned into a modern farmhouse.

Farm shops mainly sell home-produced, organic and local fruit, vegetables, meat and jams.

LOOK CLOSER!

Visit a farm shop. Find out what is made at the farm and what is bought in to sell.

Dairy Barn farm shop
TRADITIONAL RARE BREED MEAT

Mapping a farm

Look at this map of a dairy farm.
Notice how:

- the farm buildings are clustered close together
- the land is divided into separate fields
- some fields are used as **pasture** for the cows
- some fields are used for growing grass for hay, to feed the cows in winter

▼ Sheds

◀ Feeding station

▼ Milking parlour

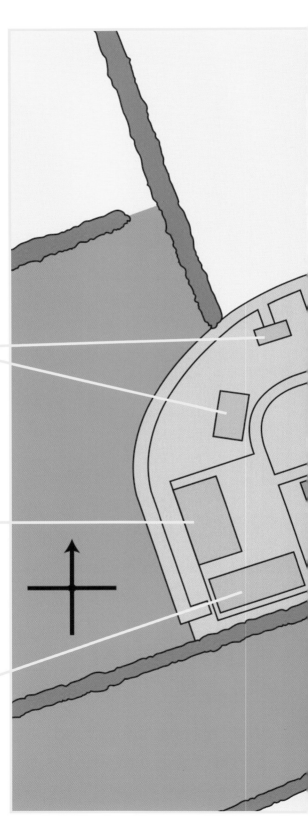

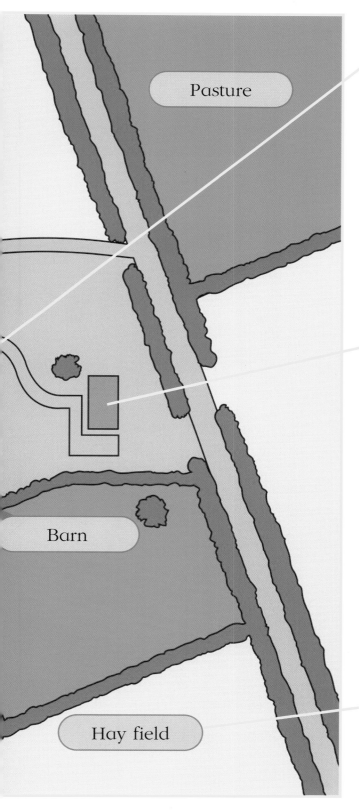

Pasture

Barn

Hay field

Farm shop

Modern farmhouse

Making hay

A walk around a farm

Farms differ widely, depending on where they are in Britain and whether they grow crops or raise animals.

When you visit a farm, notice:
- what buildings there are
- what machines the farmer uses
- what animals the farmer keeps

▲ An old thatched barn

Buildings

Several buildings make up a farm. These include a farmhouse and sheds for tools, machinery, crop storage and animals.

▲ Modern sheds

▲ This Yorkshire farm has a barn attached to the farmhouse, as well as cottages for farm workers, animal sheds and storage sheds.

Machines

Most farms have a tractor. This has attachments for different jobs.

A tractor with a trailer

A tractor with a plough

A tractor with a front-end loader for moving bales

A tractor with a grass cutter

A tractor with a sprayer

Glossary

bale a bundle of tightly tied hay

breed a particular type of animal

cattle cake a food made of barley, soya, fish meal and molasses (sugar syrup)

dipping when an animal is put in and out of a liquid very quickly

fertile soil that is fertile is full of goodness for growing crops

fertiliser something added to the soil to make crops grow better

furrow a slice of soil completely turned over by a plough

orchard an area where lots of fruit trees grow together

parasite a tiny animal that lives and feeds on another animal

pasture a field with grass for cows, sheep and other animals to eat

pest an insect that eats and spoils crops

produce food that is made

shearing clipping wool from a sheep using shears

silage winter feed for cattle made from cut, pressed grass and kept in a bale

weaned an animal is weaned when it stops drinking its mother's milk and starts eating on its own

Index